Weird and Wonderful Animals

AYE-AYES

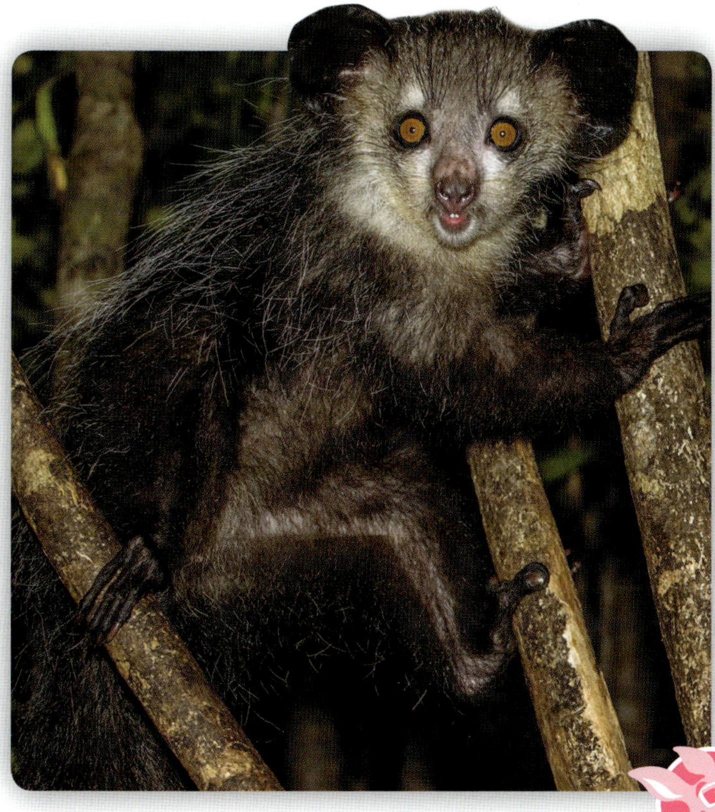

Emma Bassier

DiscoverRoo
An Imprint of Pop!
popbooksonline.com

abdobooks.com

Published by Pop!, a division of ABDO, PO Box 398166, Minneapolis, Minnesota 55439. Copyright © 2020 by POP, LLC. International copyrights reserved in all countries. No part of this book may be reproduced in any form without written permission from the publisher. Pop!™ is a trademark and logo of POP, LLC.

Printed in the United States of America, North Mankato, Minnesota.

102019
012020

THIS BOOK CONTAINS RECYCLED MATERIALS

Cover Photo: iStockphoto
Interior Photos: iStockphoto, 1, 5, 7, 8, 11, 15 (middle), 22–23, 26, 28, 31; Konrad Wothe/Minden Pictures/Newscom, 6, 27; Red Line Editorial, 9; Shutterstock Images, 12, 15 (bottom), 21, 29, 30; Martin Harvey/NHPA/Photoshot/Newscom, 13, 20; Adrian Sherratt/Alamy, 14; Wothe, K./picture alliance/Arco Images G/Newscom, 15 (top); Pete Oxford/Minden Pictures/Newscom, 17; Nick Garbutt/NHPA/Photoshot/Newscom, 18, 19; C. Lundqvist/picture alliance/blickwinkel/C/Newscom, 25

Editor: Nick Rebman
Series Designer: Jake Slavik
Library of Congress Control Number: 2019942478
Publisher's Cataloging-in-Publication Data
Names: Bassier, Emma, author.
Title: Aye-Ayes / by Emma Bassier
Description: Minneapolis, Minnesota : Pop!, 2020 | Series: Weird and wonderful animals | Includes online resources and index.
Identifiers: ISBN 9781532166037 (lib. bdg.) | ISBN 9781644943335 (pbk.) | ISBN 9781532167355 (ebook)
Subjects: LCSH: Aye-aye--Juvenile literature. | Primates--Juvenile literature. | Oddities--Juvenile literature. | Nocturnal animals--Juvenile literature. | Lemur--Juvenile literature.
Classification: DDC 599.83--dc23

WELCOME TO
DiscoverRoo!

Pop open this book and you'll find QR codes loaded with information, so you can learn even more!

Scan this code* and others like it while you read, or visit the website below to make this book pop!

popbooksonline.com/aye-ayes

*Scanning QR codes requires a web-enabled smart device with a QR code reader app and a camera.

TABLE OF
CONTENTS

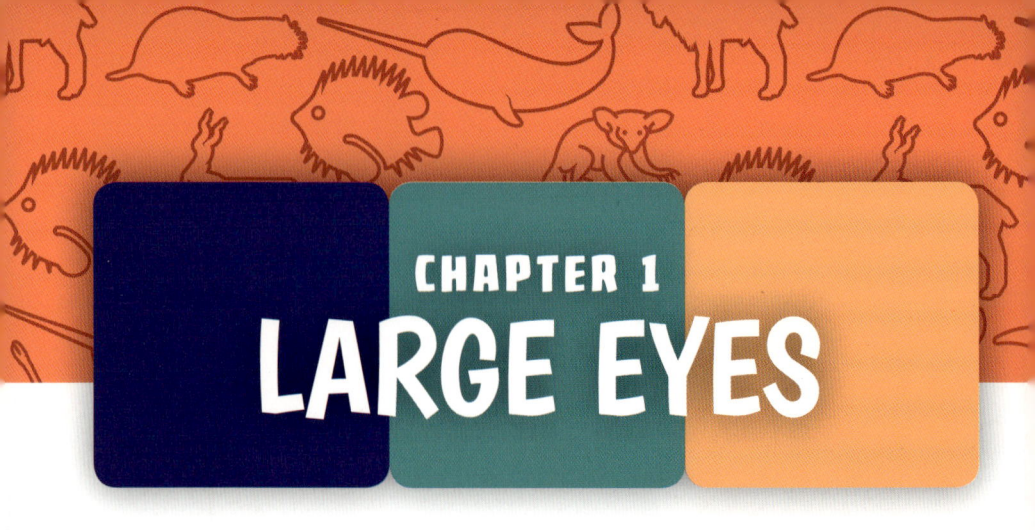

CHAPTER 1
LARGE EYES

Moonlight shines on a dark forest in Madagascar. An aye-aye opens its orange eyes. The aye-aye is hungry. It looks for food nearly all night long. Then it sleeps during the day.

WATCH A VIDEO HERE!

The aye-aye's large eyes help it see at night.

DID YOU KNOW?

Aye-ayes spend up to 80 percent of the night hunting and eating.

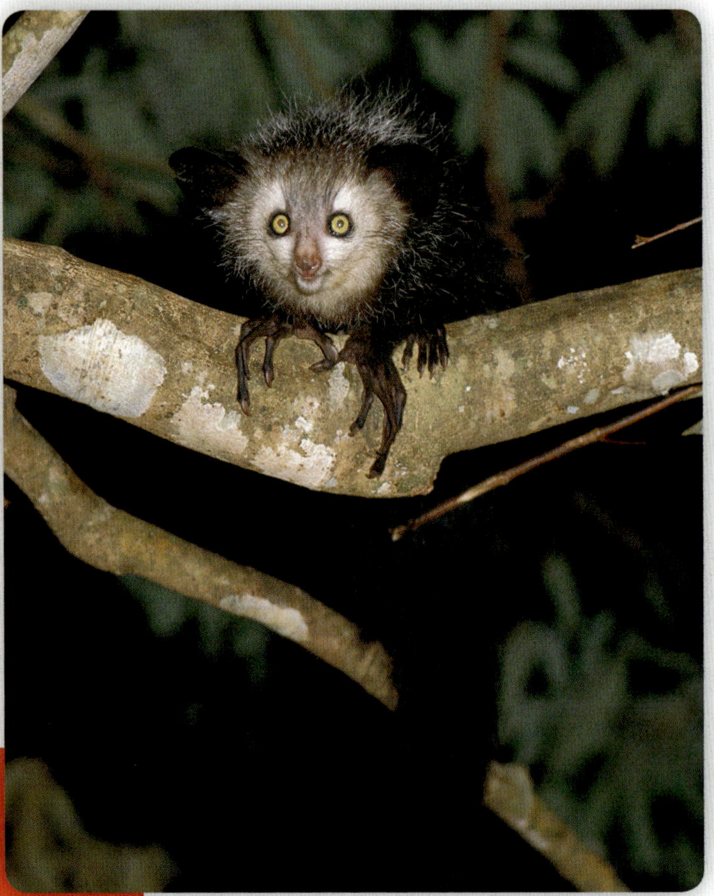

Aye-ayes are the world's largest

nocturnal primate. Primates are a type

of **mammal**. Primates have large brains,

eyes that face forward, and good vision.

They also have **opposable** thumbs or

big toes.

Gorillas are the world's largest primates.

Most of Madagascar's tropical forests are on the east coast of the country.

Aye-ayes are found only in Madagascar. They live in tropical forests. Seeing them in the wild is rare. Scientists usually guess where aye-ayes have been based on the marks they leave behind. Aye-ayes scratch and bite holes in trees when they hunt.

RANGE MAP

TANZANIA

MOZAMBIQUE

MADAGASCAR

INDIAN OCEAN

Aye-aye range

N
W E
S

CHAPTER 2

ONE LONG FINGER

The aye-aye is a type of **lemur**. Most aye-ayes weigh approximately 4 pounds (1.8 kg). Dark brown or black hair covers the animal's body. An aye-aye has a long, bushy tail.

LEARN MORE HERE!

An aye-aye's long tail hangs down when the animal sits on a branch.

Aye-ayes spend most of their time high up in trees.

Aye-ayes have large eyes and large

ears. They also have pointed nails and

sharp teeth. Aye-ayes have five long

fingers on each hand. The middle finger is longer than the others. It is also very skinny. Aye-ayes use this finger to grab insects and other foods.

DID YOU KNOW?

Similar to rodents, aye-ayes have front teeth that never stop growing.

The aye-aye's long fingers are helpful for getting food.

LIFE CYCLE OF AN AYE-AYE

The baby stays in the nest for a few weeks.

Females give birth to one baby every two to three years.

A young aye-aye lives with its mother for two years.

After two years, the young aye-aye can live on its own.

Most aye-ayes live for 20 years in the wild.

CHAPTER 3

TAPPING ON TREES

Aye-ayes hunt using **echolocation**. An aye-aye taps rapidly on a tree trunk with its skinny middle finger. The taps echo into the tree. Based on these echoes, the aye-aye can tell if insects are inside.

COMPLETE AN ACTIVITY HERE!

An aye-aye listens closely to figure out if insects are inside a tree.

DID YOU KNOW?

The aye-aye taps very quickly. It can move its finger three times per second.

An aye-aye tries to get insects out of a tree.

The aye-aye also puts its ears near the tree. The ears bend forward. Each ear forms a cup shape. The aye-aye listens for insect movement.

Next, the aye-aye chews a hole into the wood. It sticks its skinny middle finger into the hole until it pokes an insect. It uses its fingernail like a hook to pull the insect out.

An aye-aye's extra-long, skinny middle finger is a useful tool.

An aye-aye eats honeycomb from a nest of bees.

Aye-ayes mainly eat grubs and

insects. But they also eat seeds, fungi,

and fruit. Their sharp teeth help them

bite into hard fruits and nuts. Their skinny middle fingers can also scoop flesh out of fruit.

An aye-aye snacks on a coconut.

The aye-aye's wide eyes have a

reflective layer that helps the animal

see at night. An aye-aye also has large

An aye-aye has many adaptations that help it get food.

hands for its body size. This trait helps

the aye-aye hunt. One hand can grip a

tree while the other hand taps for food.

CHAPTER 4
PROTECTING AYE-AYES

During the day, aye-ayes curl up to sleep in trees. They rest on tree branches or in tangles of vines. Their dark fur helps them blend in with their surroundings.

LEARN MORE HERE!

An aye-aye rests in a tree.

Aye-ayes often screech to attract mates.

Like most **lemurs**, aye-ayes make several different sounds. For example, they can make birdlike screeches. They also communicate with scent.

Aye-ayes usually live alone. They

live in pairs when they mate or when a

mother is caring for her baby.

A mother aye-aye takes care of her baby.

A fossa roams the jungles of Madagascar.

Aye-ayes try to hide from fossa.

Fossa are catlike animals that hunt

aye-ayes. Humans can harm aye-ayes

too. Habitat loss and hunting are major

threats. But people are working to help aye-ayes survive. They set aside safe areas, such as national parks, for the animals to live.

HUMANS AND AYE-AYES

Some people in Madagascar cut down forests to make space for growing crops. And some people believe aye-ayes are a sign of death or bad luck. For this reason, they kill any aye-ayes they see. Other people work to help aye-ayes. For example, some zoos use **breeding** programs to increase aye-aye populations.

MAKING CONNECTIONS

TEXT-TO-SELF

Would you want to see an aye-aye? Why or why not?

TEXT-TO-TEXT

Have you read books about other animals that hunt at night? How are those animals similar to or different from aye-ayes?

TEXT-TO-WORLD

Aye-ayes face threats, but some people are taking action to help them. What other jobs involve working with animals?

GLOSSARY

breeding – the act of helping animals have babies.

echolocation – a process that uses sound waves and echoes to locate objects.

lemur – a small type of mammal that lives in trees.

mammal – a type of animal that has hair or fur and feeds milk to its young.

nocturnal – active at night.

opposable – able to press against other fingers for grip.

reflective – able to make light bounce off a surface.

INDEX

ONLINE RESOURCES
popbooksonline.com

Scan this code* and others like it while you read, or visit the website below to make this book pop!

popbooksonline.com/aye-ayes

*Scanning QR codes requires a web-enabled smart device with a QR code reader app and a camera.